SCHOLASTIC discover more™

Puppies and Kittens

By Penelope Arlon
and Tory Gordon-Harris

Discover even more with your free digital companion book.

woof, woof!

Fun activities!

Sounds!

Infopops!

Videos!

To download your free digital book, visit **www.scholastic.com/discovermore**

Enter this code: RM9FF22C9TX3

Contents

Literacy Consultant: Barbara Russ, 21st Century Community Learning Center Director for Winooski (Vermont) School District

Natural History Consultant: Kim Dennis-Bryan, PhD

Library of Congress Cataloging-in-Publication Data Available

ISBN 978-0-545-49566-0

10 9 8 7 6 5 4 3 2 1   13 14 15 16 17

Printed in Singapore 46
First edition, January 2013

Perfect pets

There's nothing cuter than a puppy or a kitten. And they make the best pets!

mother and puppy

Dogs are all sorts of sizes and fur lengths. It's important to choose one that's right for your family.

Always hold a puppy or kitten gently. Put one hand under its bottom and the other around its body.

A pet puppy or kitten will become a great friend!

mother and kitten

Puppies and kittens have to stay with their mothers for at least 2 months before you can take them home.

Hello, puppies

Most puppies have brothers and sisters. Puppies born at the same time form a group called a litter.

When puppies are born, their eyes are closed and they can't hear.

Dogs normally have about
3–12 puppies at a time, but
the record litter is 24!

For about 4 weeks, a puppy's only food is its mother's milk.

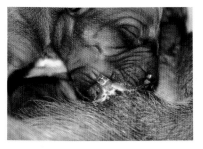

Like all mammal
mothers, female dogs
and cats make milk
inside their bodies.

While their eyes are
closed, puppies find
their way to their
mother's milk by smell.

The mother licks the
puppies to keep them
clean. This also helps
them feel safe.

Growing up

Puppies need their mothers when they are little, but before long, they are ready for play!

Puppies grow up quickly.

tired mother

A newborn pup sleeps, eats, and poops. By 2 weeks, its eyes are open.

At 3 weeks old, a puppy can hear and begins to move around.

A puppy can bark at about 2-4 weeks old. Before then, it just squeaks.

By 8 weeks, a puppy loves to chew and play. It no longer needs its mother.

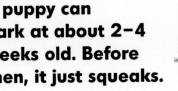

At about 4-5 weeks, a puppy has little teeth and can eat solid food.

9

Woof!

Puppies can't talk, but you can tell how they feel by watching them.

Woof! A puppy barks when it is excited, or if it wants your attention.

Wag! When a puppy is happy to see you, it wags its tail.

Roll over! A puppy rolls onto its back if it wants to be your friend.

When a puppy crouches with its bottom in the air, it wants to play.

If a puppy puts its head to one side, it is trying to understand something.

When a puppy puts its ears up, it is listening and concentrating.

newborn
kitten

Hello, kittens

Newborn kittens can't see, hear, or even walk.

All kittens are born with blue eyes, but some change eye color as they grow up.

All of these kittens can have a drink at the same time!

Kittens and puppies suckle, or drink their mother's milk.

After suckling, the kittens fall asleep. Mom can rest, too!

The mother licks her kittens to keep their fur clean.

Growing up

At first, kittens are tiny, but they grow up quickly!

If a mother needs to move her kitten, she carries it gently in her mouth.

Kittens purr at 2 days old!

At 1 week old, a kitten scrambles around on its tummy.

By 4 weeks old, a kitten has begun to play. It also has little teeth.

Kittens have baby teeth. They start to fall out at about 14 weeks, to let adult teeth grow.

At 8 weeks, a kitten can leave its mother and look after itself.

By 6 weeks old, a kitten is very curious. It loves to explore.

Meow!

Kittens are very good at showing what they want and how they feel.

A happy kitten purrs—it makes a rumbling sound in its throat.

A kitten licks you to say "I love you." Kittens have rough tongues.

Tail up! This means that the kitten is confident and happy.

This kitten is curious. Its ears are forward and its eyes are alert.

If a kitten is frightened, it fluffs up its fur and makes a hissing sound.

When a kitten shows you its tummy, it means that it trusts you.

One reason a kitten meows is when it wants something, like a stroke!

Playtime puppy!

There's nothing puppies love more than to play with one another— and with you!

It's important for a puppy to have toys so that it doesn't chew yours!

Encourage a puppy to play by showing it its toys.

Play pulling and throwing games with your puppy.

Don't be surprised if your puppy falls asleep—play is tiring!

tugging toy

ball

squeaky toy

Let's play kitten!

Kittens learn through play,
and they love it, too!

Kittens learn how to hunt by playing. A toy mouse is good practice.

Trail yarn across the floor, and watch a kitten pounce!

A kitten needs lots of sleep, so if it dozes off, you can play again later.

By playing with one another, kittens learn to jump, balance, climb, and pounce!

Training time

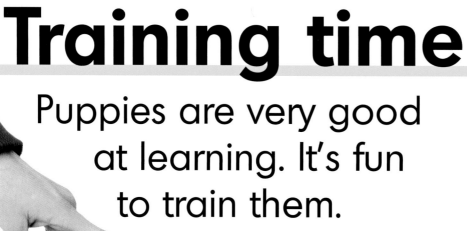

treat

Puppies are very good at learning. It's fun to train them.

lie down

Train your puppy to lie down. Give it a treat and say "good dog" when it gets it right.

sit

roll over!

Train your puppy to sit when you ask it to.

Puppies are good at learning tricks, like rolling over!

toy

leash

Train your puppy to wear a leash when you're out and about to keep it safe.

Puppy collection

Dogs come in all shapes and sizes.
Types of dog are called breeds.

beagle

Bernese
mountain
dog

miniature
dachshund

spaniel

Labrador/
boxer mix

poodle

terrier

mutt (a mixed-
breed dog)

Labrador
retriever

24

labradoodle

pug

Siberian husky

Belgian Tervuren

retriever

bulldog

long-haired dachshund

German shepherd

bulldog

Pekingese

Jack Russell terrier

25

Kitten collection

Different breeds of kitten are often similar sizes. But they have different coats.

Chartreux

American shorthair

Siamese

ragdoll

Devon rex

Scottish fold

American curl

Burmese

Sphynx

Persian

Peterbald

Kurilian bobtail

Siamese

Maine coon

Abyssinian

Persian

Sphynx

Wild cousins

Puppies and kittens have many wild relatives.

Wolf

Dogs are related to wolves. Wolves live in families called packs. Wolf pups love to play.

Wild dog

African wild dogs are about the same size as German shepherds. They have very big ears.

Lots of kittens are striped, just like tigers are. Tigers live in forests in Asia.

Leopard

Leopards are big cats that are very good at climbing trees, just like our pet cats are.

Lion

Lion cubs are like big kittens. Their play teaches them how to hunt.

Glossary

African wild dog
The largest type of African dog. It is sometimes called a painted dog because of its colorful coat.

baby tooth
A first tooth in baby mammals, sometimes called a milk tooth. Baby teeth eventually fall out and are replaced by adult teeth.

breed
A particular type of animal. Animals of the same breed have the same physical features.

coat
The fur of an animal, such as a dog or cat. Only mammals have fur.

cub
The young of some animals, such as big cats.

leopard
A large, spotted member of the cat family. It lives in Africa and Asia.

lion
A large member of the cat family. It lives in Africa and India.

litter
A number of baby animals that are born at the same time and to the same mother.

mammal
A warm-blooded animal. Mammals feed milk to their young and usually have hair. Dogs, cats, and humans are mammals.

newborn
Just born, or very recently born.

pack
An organized group
of animals that live
and work together.

pet
A tame animal kept
by humans as a
companion.

pounce
To jump down
on something,
especially when
trying to capture it.

purr
A low, rumbling
sound made by a
happy cat.

suckle
To drink milk from a
mother animal.

tiger
The largest member
of the cat family.
It lives in Asia and
has a golden coat,
with black or
brown stripes.

wag
To wave
from side
to side.
Dogs
wag
their tails
when they
are happy.

wolf
A wild dog.
The gray wolf
is the ancestor
of the pet dog.

Index

Thank you

Art Director: Bryn Walls
Designer: Ali Scrivens
Managing Editor: Miranda Smith
Managing Production Editor: Stephanie Engel
US Editor: Esther Lin
Cover Designer: Neal Cobourne
DTP: John Goldsmid
Visual Content Project Manager: Diane Allford-Trotman
**Executive Director of
Photography, Scholastic:** Steve Diamond

Photography
1: Juniors Bildarchiv/Alamy; 3: DedMorozz/iStockphoto; 4–5 (grass and sky background): anankkml/Fotolia; 4–5 (floorboards background): Petrov Stanislav Eduardovich/Shutterstock; 4l, 4r, 5tl: Isselee/Dreamstime; 5tc: Fotolia; 5tr: iStockphoto; 5bl: Thinkstock; 5br: iStockphoto; 6–7 (background t): javarman/Shutterstock; 6–7 (background b): Jagodka/Dreamstime; 6tl: iStockphoto; 7t, 7c: Thinkstock; 7br: Anke Van Wyk/Dreamstime; 7bc: iStockphoto; 7br: Arnd Rockser/Dreamstime; 8: iStockphoto; 9tr: Jagodka/Shutterstock; 9cl: iStockphoto; 9cm: T.M.O.Pets/Alamy; 9cr: TracieGrant/Shutterstock; 9bc: Ian Williams/Alamy; 10–11 (background): Fotolia; 10 (two puppies c): Thinkstock; 10bl: iStockphoto; 10bc, 10br, 10–11 (five puppies), 11 (mother dog), 11 (sleeping puppy c): Thinkstock; 11bl, 11bc, 11br: iStockphoto; 12tl: Vaaka/Dreamstime; 12: Paradoks_blizanaca/Dreamstime; 13tr: iStockphoto; 13c: Nataliya Lukhanina/Dreamstime; 13bl: Immagy/Dreamstime; 13bc: Orhan Cam/Shutterstock; 13br: Danilo Ascione/Dreamstime; 14 (background t): Thinkstock; 14 (background b): Petrov Stanislav Eduardovich/Shutterstock; 14: DK Limited/Corbis; 15tr: iStockphoto; 15cl: Thinkstock; 15cm: Sinelyov/Shutterstock; 15cr: Tony Campbell/Shutterstock; 15bc: GK Hart/Vikki Hart/Getty Images; 16–17: Fotosearch/Getty Images; 16c: Thinkstock; 16bl: iStockphoto; 16bc: Thinkstock; 16br, 17tr, 17bl, 17bc, 17br: iStockphoto; 18–19: PJ Taylor/Getty Images; 18bl, 18bc: iStockphoto; 18br: Brberrys/Shutterstock; 19tl, 19tc, 19tr: iStockphoto; 20–21: Martin Ruegner/Getty Images; 21tl, 21tc: Thinkstock; 21tr: GK Hart/Vikki Hart/Getty Images; 22tr, 22l, 22c, 22br: Thinkstock; 23l: Jose Luis Pelaez, Inc./Blend Images/Corbis; 23tc: iStockphoto; 23tr: Thinkstock; 24–25 (background): Petrov Stanislav Eduardovich/Shutterstock; 24 (beagle, Bernese mountain dog, dachshund): Erik Lam/Shutterstock; 24 (spaniel): Thinkstock; 24–25 (Labrador/boxer, labradoodle, pug, Siberian husky, Belgian Tervuren, retriever), 24 (terrier, mutt): Erik Lam/Shutterstock; 24 (poodle): VitCOM Photo/Shutterstock; 24–25 (Labrador retriever, bulldog l, dachshund, German shepherd, bulldog r): Erik Lam/Shutterstock; 25 (Pekingese, Jack Russell terrier): iStockphoto; 26–27 (background): Petrov Stanislav Eduardovich/Shutterstock; 26 (American shorthair): DAJ/Getty Images; 26 (Siamese), 26 (ragdoll), 26 (Chartreux), 26 (Devon rex), 26 (Scottish fold), 26 (American curl), 26 (Burmese), 27tr, 27 (Sphynx t), 27 (Persian t), 27 (Peterbald), 27 (Kurilian bobtail), 27 (Siamese), 27 (Maine coon), 27 (Abyssinian): Thinkstock; 27 (Sphynx b): iStockphoto; 27 (Persian b): Thinkstock; 28–29: Aditya "Dicky" Singh/Alamy; 28l, 28bl, 28br: Thinkstock; 29c: Eric Isselée/Shutterstock; 29bl, 29br: Thinkstock; 30, 31: Thinkstock; 32: iStockphoto.

Cover
Background: (bone) Dreamstime; (kitten) iStockphoto. Front cover: (tl) Kubangirl/Dreamstime; (tr) Cynoclub/Dreamstime; (c) Tim Davis/Corbis. Back cover: (computer monitor) Manaemedia/Dreamstime.